W9-BFO-652

TANA HOBAN

I Read Signs

Macmillan/McGraw-Hill School Publishing Company
New York   Chicago   Columbus

This one
is for
all my
children

With many thanks
to the sign-finders

Macmillan/McGraw-Hill School Division
10 Union Square East
New York, New York 10003

Printed in the United States of America

ISBN 0-02-179053-1 / K, U.8

5 6 7 8 9 BCM 99 98 97

SCHOOL
SPEED LIMIT 15

6

BEWARE OF DOG

DO NOT ENTER

EXIT ONLY

FIRE HOSE

11

RAILROAD CROSSING

14

NO LEFT TURN

NO STANDING

EXPRESS

DEPT OF TRANSPORTATION

BIKE ROUTE

26

DEAD END

TOWN OF BRIGHTON